W9-CBT-666

Left or Right?

Susan Markowitz Meredith

ROURKE
PUBLISHING
www.rourkepublishing.com

www.rourkepublishing.com

PHOTO CREDITS: Cover: © Dubravko Grakalíc; Title Page: © Bart Broek; Page 3, 8, 12, 16, 20: © Alexandr Marakov; Page 4: © Charles Harton; Page 5: © infomages; Page 7, 8, 9, 11, 12, 15, 16, 17, 19, 20: © Craig Lopetz; Page 13: © Jaimie Duplass; Page 21: © Zsöllér Ervin; Page 23: © Jasmin Merdan

Edited by Kelli L. Hicks

Cover and Interior design by Tara Raymo

Library of Congress Cataloging-in-Publication Data

Merideth, Susan.
 Left or right / Susan Merideth.
    p. cm. -- (Little world math concepts)
 Includes bibliographical references and index.
 ISBN 978-1-61590-290-3 (Hard Cover) (alk. paper)
 ISBN 978-1-61590-529-4 (Soft Cover)
 1. Left and right (Psychology)--Juvenile literature. I. Title.
 BF637.L36M47 2011
 152.3'35--dc22
                               2010009611

Rourke Publishing
Printed in the United States of America, North Mankato, Minnesota
020111
01312011LP-A

www.rourkepublishing.com - rourke@rourkepublishing.com
Post Office Box 643328 Vero Beach, Florida 32964

Left   Right

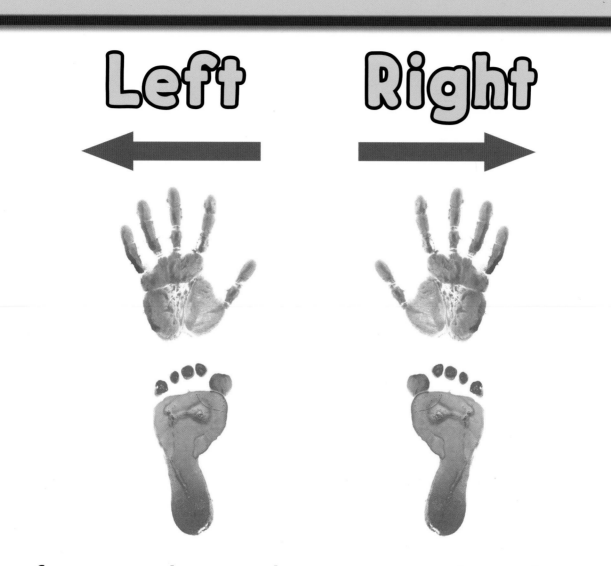

Left or right? Where is each side?

The **left** page has swings.

The **right** page has a slide.

Right or left?

Which way is the boy turning?

Right

He's turning to the **right**.

Left or right?

Which shoe is untied?

Right

The **right** one needs tying.

My shoes
are tied.
Let's play!

13

Right or left?

Which arm reaches high?

Left

Her **left** arm reaches high.

Left or right?

Which way are the children looking?

Right

They look to their **right**. Why?

Come and get your ice cream!

Yummy! Hold on tight!

Which hand holds the treats?
Left or **right**?

Index

Websites

pbskids.org/curiousgeorge/games/feed_gnocchi/feed_gnocchi.html

pbskids.org/cyberchase/webisode_3/web_game3.html

macmillanmh.com/math/2003/student/activity/courses/grk/ch01b/

www.meddybemps.com/9.691.html

About the Author

Susan Markowitz Meredith uses left and right all the time. She writes with her left hand and bowls with her right. She keeps socks in her left drawer and gym clothes in her right. Knowing the difference between left and right makes her life much easier.